Victoria

The ART of COLLECTING

Personal Treasures That Make a Home

Victoria

The ART of
COLLECTING

Personal Treasures That Make a Home

FROM THE EDITORS OF *VICTORIA*

83
PRESS

Hoffman Media
1900 International Park Drive, Suite 50
Birmingham, Alabama 35243
hoffmanmedia.com

ISBN 978-0-9785489-2-6
Printed in USA

83
PRESS

SÈVRES

CONTENTS

INTRODUCTION

I T MAY START WITH JUST ONE SPECIAL PIECE THAT CATCHES your eye and captures your heart, stirring an affection that quickly grows into an assemblage so dear, its sentimental value is beyond calculation. Whether it is a passion for exquisite linens, sterling silver, or fine English china—or simply the thrill of the hunt—that entices us to sift through old attics and antiques shops, estate sales, and European *brocantes*, we are kindred spirits, linked by an unbridled fervor for curating our favorite things.

This volume brims with page after page of the variety of heirlooms that have featured in *Victoria* magazine since the very first issue. From dainty cameos and samples of delicate lace to architectural fragments and hand-carved furniture, countless treasures draw our attention with their beauty and provenance. This pretty parade of compositions promises both a visual treat and a cache of valuable information, with wisdom and inspiration offered in equal measure from esteemed antiques vendors and impassioned collectors. Demonstrating the warmth of patina that timeworn objects lend to interiors, homeowners invite us into spaces adorned with prized bibelots. In artful vignettes, find ideas for displaying your own cherished items and all the unexpected curios yet to come.

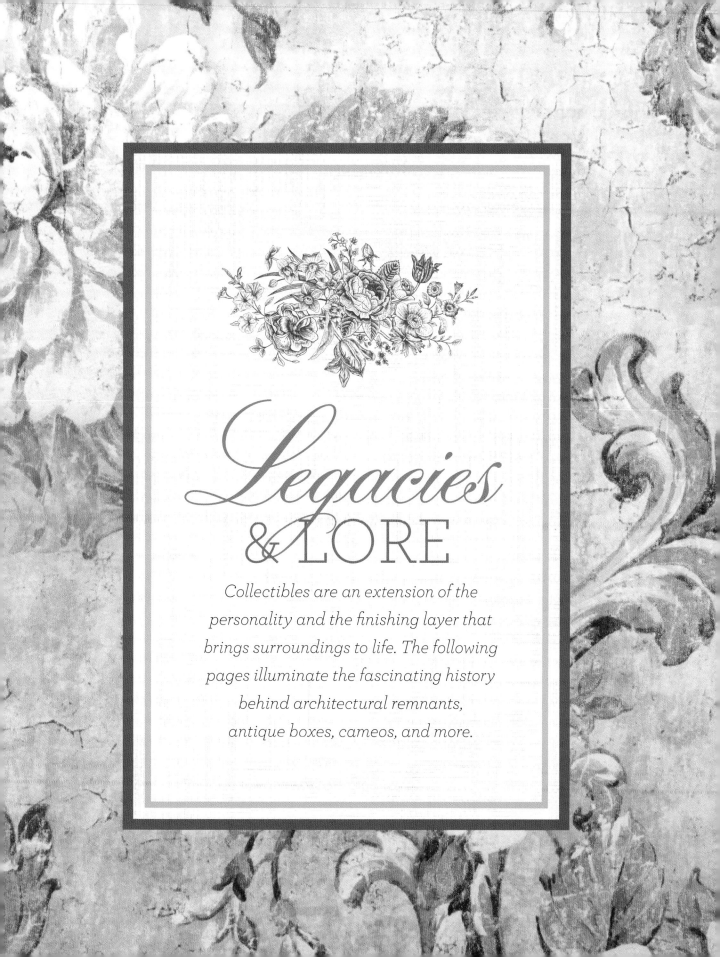

Legacies & LORE

Collectibles are an extension of the personality and the finishing layer that brings surroundings to life. The following pages illuminate the fascinating history behind architectural remnants, antique boxes, cameos, and more.

PIECES OF THE PAST

Weathered objects hold a certain fascination, offering a tactile connection to times experienced only through the pages of books. Write the next chapter by assimilating these cherished remnants into home design.

The legendary markets and fairs of France are veritable meccas for antiques hunters, who patiently sift through the seemingly endless mélange of wares in search of hidden treasure. Some of the most coveted items are salvaged architectural fragments—tangible emblems of the country's long and fascinating narrative.

There are many ways to incorporate these enduring gems into home décor. Hand-carved wooden panels can be found in a range of sizes, making them perfect accents to hang over a mantel, fill a blank wall, serve as a headboard, or to create a decorative apron for the front of a desk. Smaller remnants add aesthetic elements to frames and mingle with other curios in bookcases.

Pedestals are also favored relics utilized in interior design. These can be fashioned into lamps or used to display art or floral arrangements. Luxurious tapestries evoke a sense of history and often inspire the color

scheme for a room. Architectural sketches, matted and framed, are ideal in a study or a library, as are antique books. Volumes made with vellum and bound in animal-skin covers are precious finds, especially if the text is in Latin.

Ancient churches are a common source for many of these timeworn bits and pieces: Crumbling altars offer exquisitely carved cherubs, pillars, and more. Gold leaf, usually applied over a gesso base, was often chosen for embellishment; the inevitable age-related chipping and peeling does nothing to diminish the desirability of the fragments and, in fact, increases their appeal.

New Life
FOR OLD SILVER

Antique silver cases offer a dainty substitute for a classic wallet and are the perfect size to hold pocketbook necessities—credit cards, driver's license, and a bit of cash. These meticulously decorated cases are traditionally cherished as collectibles, but they are too lovely to be relegated to a storage box. Why not turn one into a stylish yet practical accessory?

In the 1920s, there were few things so fashionable and glamorous as a sterling cigarette case. Next to elbow-length gloves or an incredibly long strand of pearls, a beautiful silver case was a sure sign of an alluring woman.

Cases differed slightly from one piece to the next—some were flat and square, while others were oblong and rounded to fit the gentle curve of a lady's hand. Several were made of papier-mâché or wood, but the most treasured were those crafted of sterling silver.

"The ornate sterling cases were expertly decorated," says Karyn Shaudis, former proprietor of Nightingale Antiques in Bakersfield, California. They were as highly regarded as fine jewelry, and surfaces were often embellished with engraved monograms, hand-chased patterns, inset semiprecious stones, and mother-of-pearl accents. "They were often quite elaborate," says Karyn.

Some cases date to the mid-1800s and were originally used to hold calling cards, a hallmark of Victorian social culture. By the era of the flapper and the Charleston, women had repurposed some of these antique cases to hold mirrors, cigarettes, cake blush, and spare coins.

In the same vein as using a treasured heirloom piece for a more modern purpose, many women now use the slender cigarette cases as an alternative to a wallet to carry business cards and other pocketbook essentials. The quiet glamour of these lovely pieces adds a romantic, vintage element to the everyday.

Enduring
IRONSTONE

Born in England nearly two centuries ago, this earthenware immigrant continues to delight collectors the world over with its gleaming finish, clean lines, and charming designs.

English white ironstone has been tickling the fancy of Americans with its decidedly "unfancy" appeal since it was first imported and fervently acquired in the nineteenth century. Now a chic antique, the gleaming all-white earthenware has a goes-with-anything simplicity and a fits-in-anywhere charm that elicits as much pleasure among modern-day collectors as when it graced the tables of colonists, pioneers, and Victorians centuries ago.

Introduced by Staffordshire potters as a durable, affordable substitute for porcelain, the earliest incarnations of the dense, heavy stoneware were colorfully decorated. But when unadorned white ironstone garnered instant favor in America for everyday use, its popularity inspired a heyday of mass production from 1840 to 1870.

Ever since the era in which English white ironstone made its way across the ocean, the sturdy stuff has remained an accessible, sought-after prize. To this day, its many collectors continue to scour tag sales, antiques markets, and online auctions in search of the perfect teapot, gravy boat, or tureen to treasure.

FOR THE COLLECTOR

Sleek white ironstone enhances almost any décor—from cottage to country, traditional to contemporary. With its two-hundred-year history, selecting pieces for authenticity and quality can be daunting. Below are some helpful tips for those who wish to add these timeless treasures to their repertoire.

SPOTTING THE REAL THING

❥ The ability to identify English ironstone comes with experience and knowledge, as well as a practiced eye. Some pieces bear a distinguishing mark, although others do not. Color also provides clues about age and origin: Newer American-made ironstone appears creamy white when compared with earlier, authentic English pieces that possess a snowy white or barely blue-gray hue. When American potters took up producing all-white wares in the late nineteenth century, English pottery sold less extensively.

BEGINNING A COLLECTION

❥ Hardy and hospitable dinnerware, tea services, chamber sets, and other utilitarian white ironstone fulfilled nineteenth-century Americans' dreams of pristine table settings and home embellishments. Today, particular patterns or pieces evoke the passions of many collectors seeking something specific to match great-grandmother's relish dish. Others acquire less-than-perfect examples that simply appeal for their potential. Researching ironstone in books and online can be useful for determining which kinds are most intriguing.

Delicate Cameos

Since ancient times, artisans have carved intricate designs into everything from shells and stones to fine metals and precious gems to create the exquisite images that continue to enchant collectors with their enduring beauty.

With origins reaching back to the earliest days of Roman, Grecian, and Egyptian cultures, glyptic carving, a term which refers to cameos and intaglios, is an art form that is as timeless as it is beautiful. From delicate flowers etched on glass to historical figures chiseled in stone, the variety of subjects and mediums is seemingly endless.

Although similar in appearance, there is a distinct difference between these two forms. *Cameo* refers to a relief image raised from its background, whereas an intaglio has an indented appearance, made by carving into the material. Both methods produce detailed depictions that have won favor for centuries.

Known for their feminine motifs, cameos often feature in women's jewelry, placed on a necklace, a bracelet, or a pair of earrings. They were considered the perfect accessory in the Edwardian era, when ladies pinned cameo brooches in the center of the high lace collars that were fashionable in that period.

The cozy Manhattan boutique of Italian artisan Amedeo Scognamiglio includes a lively blend of custom handcrafted pieces, with designs that range from traditional to contemporary. A sardonyx cameo belt buckle with Sardinian coral and freshwater pearls nestles between classically inspired objects, such as a shell paperweight dipped in sterling silver.

Cameos are also found in an assortment of decorative items, such as beautiful Wedgwood china. Elise Abrams, proprietor of Elise Abrams Antiques in Great Barrington, Massachusetts, has many fine examples of these objects among the offerings in her shop, such as knife rests, nut dishes, and her personal favorite to collect, place card holders.

As beloved as ever, these decorative compositions instill a dainty yet dignified element wherever they appear—a reminder that true artistry and elegance never go out of style.

THE *Allure* OF ANTIQUE BOXES

An intriguing blend of artistry and practicality, these versatile remnants of times past have been sought for centuries as trusted repositories for everything from tea to trinkets. Whether simply clad in unadorned wood or embellished with inlaid mother-of-pearl designs, they pique our curiosity about what lies within.

Like a lovingly wrapped gift, antique boxes beckon with exteriors featuring brass scrollwork, hand-painted floral motifs, and elaborate marquetry. Occasionally filled with timeworn accessories that hint of their past, the interiors can be every bit as delightful.

"Today, boxes are collected as decorative pieces, but when they first became commonly used in the eighteenth century, they had a more practical purpose," says Barbara Ashford, who is the co-proprietor of Birmingham, Alabama–based shop Ashford Hill for Henhouse Antiques— a treasure trove of fine antique European boxes and other elegant furnishings. "They were used to store various objects like important papers, tea, sewing supplies, and toiletries. Each was handcrafted and unique."

So prized were their contents that many of these vessels were fitted with locks. When tea was introduced in England in the late seventeenth century, it was an expensive commodity. Those who were wealthy enough to afford it stored the leaves in lockable wooden boxes, which became known as tea caddies. The lady of the house often kept the caddy key on a chatelaine around her waist so that overly curious servants would not be tempted to pilfer the bounty within the container.

Similar to tea caddies, writing boxes—also known as lap desks—typically came equipped with locks and keys for keeping their contents safe. These portable offices, which typically revealed a foldout writing slope for penning correspondence, were carried great distances on sea voyages and military campaigns. Many also offered handy

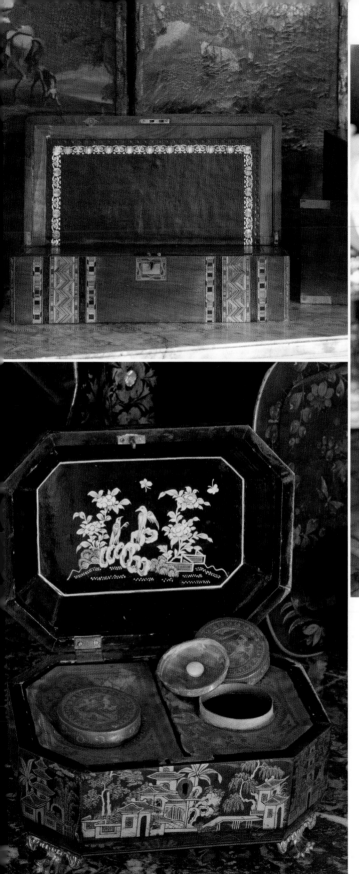

compartments for writing essentials such as glass inkwells and sealing wax.

"I think of antique boxes as beautiful works of art," says Barbara, who handpicks the ones for her shop with her business partner, Judy Hill, on their buying trips to England each year. "Some even harbor a delightful surprise with secret drawers and compartments."

Cherished for their decorative charms, antique boxes continue to enchant, whether tucked amid books on a shelf or carefully placed in a tableau of mementos on a tabletop. "When I think about accessorizing an outfit, what really makes it wonderful is that little piece of jewelry, and that's what antique boxes do," Barbara says. "They add that finishing touch that makes a room special."

INFUSED WITH HISTORY

Hand-crafted with an array of artistic compositions, tea caddies offer a fascinating glimpse into rituals of old.

➤ The first tea containers were of humble origin—jars made of affordable porcelain or faïence, often produced in beloved blue-and-white colorways. To match the costly assets of the leaves they housed, soon these utilitarian boxes gave way to more ornamental receptacles constructed of opulent materials, such as tortoiseshell, brass, and pewter; more common were finely wrought wooden chests crafted with rosewood, mahogany, and satinwood. Diverse designs, from rare fruit-shaped caddies, shown center right, to intricately fashioned boxes adorned with gilded rolled paper, above left, exhibit a unique sense of culture and creative talent dating back to the eighteenth century. Secret interior chambers are thought to have housed silver teaspoons and sugar. Below right: A double-compartment caddy features a jasperware plaque depicting dancing nymphs.

THE *Luster* OF PEWTER

With a more subdued gleam than its silver sister, the malleable blend of tin, copper, and antimony known as pewter has been used through the ages for crafting everything from cups to candlesticks.

L ong before people were setting tables with porcelain plates and sipping from crystal glasses, they were creating multipurpose dinnerware from pewter. With a low melting point ideal for casting in moulds, the tin-based alloy was a favorite of craftsmen as far back as the Bronze Age. The oldest known piece, dating to 1450 BC, was discovered in an Egyptian tomb.

Though the early products were composed of tin and lead, James Vickers of Sheffield, England, discovered in 1769 that replacing the lead with touches of copper and antimony resulted in a stronger product. Known as Britannia metal, the new formula could be spun, rolled, and pressed, opening the door to mass production and greater distribution to the public. All tiers of society, from royalty to the working class, were enamored with this sturdy, and less costly, alternative to silver, which was fashioned in items as common as pub tankards and as lofty as ecclesiastical chalices.

America did not have the available sources of tin found in England; therefore, Colonial pewterers plied their trade by either repairing broken or dented British pieces or by melting and recasting them. American artisans eschewed ornamentation, relying instead on simple lines to give the objects character. Because so few Revolution-era tankards exist today, they are considered rare finds, with price tags that reflect their value to collectors.

Many lovely examples of antique pewter can still be found, though it is often difficult to distinguish British from American-made, as Colonial craftsmen frequently used British moulds. The pieces may be used in service, bearing in mind that older ones usually contain some percentage of lead. Few have maker's marks, but all of these timeworn treasures have the lustrous patina that makes pewter collectibles attractive for displaying in homes.

THE CARE AND CLEANING OF PEWTER

Although it is best to leave the restoration of valuable pieces to professionals, here are some tips for keeping a collection in prime condition.

➤ Pewter does not tarnish like silver, but it acquires a patina that can range from muted silver to charcoal gray. Many pieces merely need wiping down with a sponge dipped in warm, soapy water. Then rinse and dry with a soft cloth.

➤ Be sure to clean any sediment after use to avoid pitting.

➤ Darkened pieces may be brightened with an all-purpose metal polish.

➤ Some collectors prefer the deeper patina that comes with age. In this case, periodic dusting is all that is required.

TO *Have*
AND TO HOLD

*Long after a ring has been passed down to
younger hands, the container which
both protected the jewel and mirrored its
magnificence remains as a memento to its tale.*

For collector Courtney Hildebrand, there is magic in a sterling ring box. The precious metal, which she's gathered for decades, is familiar to her, like the smile of an old friend. Stories that each piece could share, however, are a mystery she constantly pursues.

"It looks like a piece of candy to me," Courtney says. She discovered the collectible in the pages of *Victoria* magazine before procuring her first at a Memphis flea market. To this day, that initial find is her most precious. Manufactured by Birks, the standard-setter of Canadian jewelry, this 1930s antique was marked with a Royal Warrant of Appointment from the Prince of Wales—an indication of the royal family's patronage, which makes the box all the more valuable.

Most of Courtney's collection dates to the early twentieth century and hails from America, Canada,

or England. When she searches, she aspires to curate variety among her pieces. They may be round, square, or heart-shaped, with a vibrant velvet or satin lining in shades of emerald, ruby, or even eggplant. The handcrafted interior indicates the care artisans took in creating each box long ago, as well as the love imbued by its owner over the many years since.

To protect the silver from tarnishing, Courtney advises collectors to enclose the boxes behind glass, as too much polishing can fade any engravings over time. These inscriptions are often the only way to verify the item's origin, though some pieces are unmarked, and others still were engraved for personal reasons long after their original use. Although much of the provenance of sterling ring boxes remains a mystery, Courtney fervently researches in libraries and online forums, aiming to spread her knowledge to antiques lovers around the world.

SÈVRES

Cité de la CÉRAMIQUE

Taking their inspiration from pieces produced by an esteemed French porcelain manufactory, antique prints and exquisite china mingle elegantly, evocative of the luxury enjoyed by many nobles throughout the ages.

Named for the French town in which it resides, Sèvres became known as the standard-setter for European porcelain following its debut in 1740, supported in its early days by notable patrons King Louis XV and his most influential mistress, Madame de Pompadour. The two were so fond of the hand-painted wares that they placed the business under full control of the crown and built its factory near her Château de Bellevue. In honor of the king, many older specimens are marked on the base by two interlaced *L*s in blue script.

Sèvres entered into the realm of academia with the creation of the Ceramic and Glass Museum. Today, the cache boasts fifty thousand works, including illustrations that replicate the brand's best artifacts. Originally painted by Édouard Garnier, curator of the museum until his death in 1903, these chromolithographs were published in his prized 1892 book, *The Soft Porcelain of Sèvres*, which chronicled the company's history of quality and innovation.

Collectors can find authentic prints and items of antique porcelain through private sellers, or they may peruse the manufactory's suburban museum and Paris showroom. In addition, modern interpretations of iconic pieces demonstrate the timeless beauty, exceptional artistry, and enduring appeal of designs conceived long ago.

Flourished
IN GOLD

The distinctive style of decorative arts that began in fourteenth-century Italy may have its roots in Florence, but its timeless allure reaches far beyond the Tuscan borders.

Known as the birthplace of the Renaissance, Florence, Italy, has long enjoyed its reputation as a center for art. Florentine artists such as Raphael and Michelangelo created brilliantly hued and meticulously detailed paintings, most often with ecclesiastical themes, and gold leaf was used liberally, especially to denote sacred figures.

Local craftsmen began making their own interpretations of this ornate style in the form of triptychs, picture frames, and furniture. As interest for these pieces grew, the community craft guilds provided crucial support to these artisans, ensuring they could keep up with the demand and that the desire for their products would continue for centuries. These items were particularly favored by British tourists during the Victorian era, allowing them to bring souvenirs of the continent home from their travels.

Florentine-style wooden trays and boxes are among the highly sought-after collectibles bearing the imprint of these Italian Renaissance artists. Often employing inlays

or a découpage technique, the pieces may depict historical or religious scenes, or they might feature one emblem or design; others may be decorated in a simple repeating pattern, such as checkerboard or diamonds. All are characteristically trimmed in gold leaf or paint.

Trays are found in many sizes and shapes, from small rounds to large ovals, as well as in square and hexagonal forms. Edges are often scalloped for an extra touch of elegance. Boxes also come in a variety of dimensions, and while both trays and boxes are painted in a wide range of colors, the signature gold accents are a common thread.

Because of their unique beauty, Florentine trays make eye-catching displays when grouped together as wall art or set on easels throughout the home. Likewise, boxes look lovely tucked amid volumes on bookshelves or placed atop dressers for storing jewelry and other precious mementos.

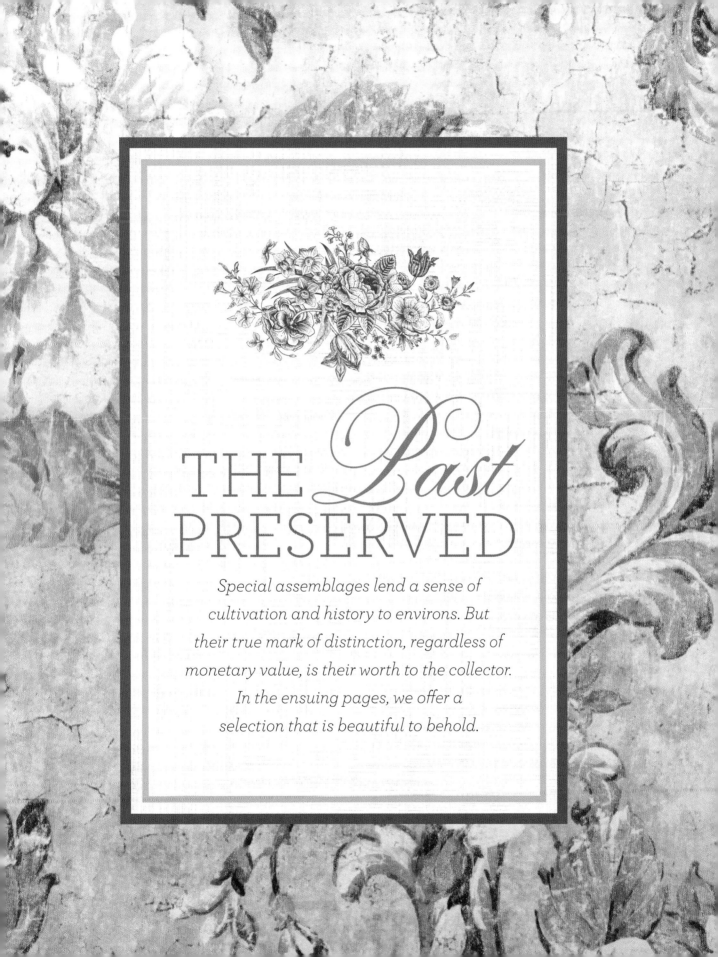

THE *Past* PRESERVED

*Special assemblages lend a sense of
cultivation and history to environs. But
their true mark of distinction, regardless of
monetary value, is their worth to the collector.
In the ensuing pages, we offer a
selection that is beautiful to behold.*

Sentimental
SOUVENIRS

One-of-a-kind collectibles from some of the world's most famous hotels glimmer with the luster and grandeur of history and romance.

On a summery evening in 1905, as awed guests of the Savoy looked on, the courtyard of London's premier hotel was transformed into a bejeweled, makeshift scene from Venice. A silk-lined gondola, flanked by snowy swans and strewn with twelve thousand carnations, made its way down a man-made canal toward those gathered while the great Caruso serenaded them—the whole of the moonlit scene gleaming in the subtle glow of hundreds of Venetian paper lanterns.

The host of the famed gondola dinner was well-known Champagne millionaire George Kessler, who managed

to top the lavish event just four years later at the Savoy with a festive $300-a-plate Yuletide feast in the Winter Garden, fashioned to resemble the North Pole.

More than one hundred years later, many of the Savoy's wonderful wares were placed on the auction block when new owners made the decision to undergo a $100 million renovation. Crystal chandeliers, mahogany chairs, saltcellars, silver salvers, teapots, and duvets were among the items offered to sentimentalists longing to own a souvenir from the hotel where Strauss conducted, Pavlova danced, and Monet painted.

While weighing the strength of the dollar versus the pound sterling, San Francisco vintages expert and antiques dealer Lynn Goldfinger savored the possibilities and set her sights high.

"My dream item would be the white grand piano used by Frank Sinatra on numerous occasions," Lynn says. "I'm a big fan of Sinatra's and saw him perform live a couple of times. What a thrill to own that piece!"

Also on Lynn's wishful Savoy bid list: silver platters, china, and octagonal wine tables, some for her own collection and other pieces to pass along to clients. Through her San Francisco and web-based business,

Paris Hotel Boutique, Lynn shares her passion for the glitz and glamour of world-class hotels from eras past.

Lynn's sought-after collectibles include vintage pieces that are tied to a particular hotel with a stamp or an engraved marking, as well as others that are unique in purpose, period, and style. Through Lynn, one might find a 1930s Café de Paris oyster server, a circa 1912 eggcup from the Hotel McAlpin in New York, or a monogrammed creamer from the Savoy. And the San Francisco native's curiosity and interests are not limited to silver. With a seasoned and discerning eye, she has accrued numerous sets and individual pieces of hotel china as well.

From such destinations as the Ritz in Paris, the St. Francis, the Fairmont, the Hôtel Plaza Athénée, and the Waldorf Astoria, Lynn procures silver and china, furniture, and even key fobs and door keys. Some items are reserved for her 1939 home—where collections are set against a Dorothy Draperesque backdrop, displayed with equal parts suave sophistication and neoclassical kitsch. In one room alone, Lynn has lovingly arranged more than two hundred pieces of silver from hotels around the world. Other prizes include chairs from the magical Fairmont San Francisco's Crown Room, where Lynn recalls brunching with her family on special occasions throughout her childhood.

Most of Lynn's precious hotel finds, however, are shared with collectors of like minds—people who hunger for the ephemeral elegance of a time that has passed and a pantheon to which few were invited.

The great hotels of our time bear mute witness to some of history's most noteworthy moments—be it Tallulah Bankhead sipping Champagne from her slipper or the future Queen Elizabeth II spying her prince-to-be across a crowded dance floor. To own a keepsake from one of these majestic locales—perhaps a marmalade server, a pair of sugar tongs, or even a vintage menu—is to tap into that legacy and perhaps even become part of the story as it continues to unfold.

"I think that is what is so great about vintage versus new things. There are so many beautiful things out there that are new, but they don't have the patina, they don't have the provenance. And, most importantly," says Lynn, "they don't have the soul."

COLLECTING HOTEL SILVER

Lynn suggests these tips when plundering flea markets, jumble sales, and antiques stores for vintage hotel silver.

➤ Mix and match hollowware, serving ware, and other pieces with markings from different hotels, and display in groups throughout the home.

➤ Look for pieces that have a unique shape, raised crests, monograms, or other markings. These design details authenticate and individualize the pieces and add to their visual appeal.

➤ Don't limit collections to a specific time period or the geographic location of the hotel. Age is of lesser importance than quality when judging fine silver, such as pieces made by Reed & Barton or Gorham.

➤ If the piece is intended for serving and the interior is corroded from age, have a silversmith replate it.

Antique Lace:
A LOVELY LEGACY

From collars and handkerchiefs to curtains and
pillow slips, lace—that most delicate of adornments—
weaves the threads of history to decorate our everyday
lives, one ephemeral stitch at a time.

Through the centuries, lace has signified sheer luxury. The fancy and frilled designs of its ornamental openwork offer intricate patterns, but its romance lies in what cannot be seen.

"Whenever I touch lace, I connect with it," says Beverly Ruff, whose eponymous shop in Birmingham, Alabama, specialized in linens and lace from the nineteenth and early twentieth centuries. "I wonder who made it, where it was made, when it was made, and for whom it was made. It's the mystery that intrigues."

What blushing bride folded the dainty handkerchief around her bouquet of white roses? What holiday repast was laid out upon the lace tablecloth? And whose little head fit so snugly inside the precious baby cap ringed with snowy white eyelets?

"I want to know their stories, which have been lost in time," Beverly says. "And I want to add new chapters."

Such sentimentality lies at the heart of these keepsakes, whose creation was initially considered women's work. Lace making, which has been traced to the sixteenth century, was a cottage industry, and the first pieces were designed to adorn the vestments of Europe's nobility. Each country produced its own handmade designs until the nineteenth century, when

machine-made lace was manufactured for the middle-class market. Today, lace from the nineteenth and early twentieth centuries, although perhaps not the most collectible, is the most widely available.

Choices include Battenberg, a highly textured variety with fanciful flowers; Normandy, a patchwork of different types of French lace; needle lace, whose diaphanous design is formed from hundreds, even thousands, of small stitches; crochet lace; Alençon, the so-called Queen of Lace, which sometimes resembles snowflakes; and net, the whisper-fine lace that serves as a background for all manner of embroidered decoration.

"The real beauty of lace is that it's pretty and can be used in a variety of ways," Beverly says. "It doesn't have to be perfect, and it shows its age well. All you have to do is use your imagination."

Through her creativity, lace-topped vanity trays have become beverage-serving salvers and wall hangings, lace panels have been converted into pillows, collars have been draped artistically over cabinet shelves, mantel scarves have been fashioned into shawls, and hand-embroidered rounds have doubled as "bouquets" in bridal baskets.

Of course, one can't have lace without linens. "They go together like love and marriage," Beverly says. "I always tell people to buy lace because they love it. It's already beautiful, so all you have to do is give it new life."

Bygone BEAUTIES

Learning the ropes of antiques collecting at her mother's knee led one woman to pursue a lifelong passion for things that beckon with the rich patina of age.

Dozens of multihued crystal prisms hang from Rose Ann Kendrick's dining-room chandelier, sending showers of color across the elegantly set table. Lacy place mats hold a pyramid of gleaming gold-rimmed plates, and silverware polished to perfection rests upon pristine white napkins. Every imaginable accessory, from silver chalices and goblets encrusted with gold overlay to saltcellars and place card holders, rounds out the display. At the center of it all stands a Minton bowl-turned-vase spilling over with a profusion of mophead hydrangeas.

Rose Ann's home is filled with an eclectic assemblage of pieces that have an obvious common thread: quintessential beauty. She began accumulating these heirlooms at a very young age, starting with small china animals and the hand-painted eggs she found in her Easter basket every year. She comes by her affinity for timeworn objects honestly; one might even say it is in her genes. Her mother, an antiques collector, had a penchant for china and linens. She introduced her daughter to the wonders of overcrowded aisles teeming with treasures and of auctions where coveted prizes were won with the wave of a paddle. The pint-size protégé caught on quickly.

"I collected whatever I took a fancy to," says Rose Ann. And more often than not, the items she fancied had sweet stories attached to them. Much of her cache was inherited, such as mint green-and-gold plates from Marshall Field's and the candelabra adorning the dining room table. But most of it was discovered on the countless trips she and her mother made across the South, combing through markets from Round Top, Texas, to Palm Beach, Florida. She would find something that caught her eye—a cut-glass wine decanter or Victorian knife rests—and then soon uncover another and another until she had assembled a new bevy of beauties.

Though she recently downsized to smaller living quarters and a portion of her acquisitions now resides in storage, Rose Ann is surrounded by the exquisite things she has lovingly curated to enjoy for years to come.

ENCHANTED BY TOLEWARE

*The collection of Lidy Baars, antiques dealer and proprietor
of French Garden House, delights both decorators and collectors.*

Alluring, hand-painted metal trays, urns, and baskets cast a spell of history and the romance of bygone days. Painted with great skill, these prized collectibles are both decorative and functional, and typically feature floral or Eastern motifs.

Toleware refers to objects, dating from 1600 to 1900, made of tinned metal lacquered and adorned with designs. John Hanbury, who began his metalware business in the Welsh town of Pontypool in the 1600s, is credited with inventing the method of japanning. This process is used to alleviate rust on metal by coating the painted surface with a mixture of asphalt and shellac resembling the glossy lacquer finish on Japanese trays. Distinguished by lacy, openwork rims, Pontypool trays continue to be some

of the most sought-after tole pieces. The French developed their own interpretations that boast brightly colored backgrounds and a variety of decorations.

By the early to mid-1700s, painted tin was being manufactured in England and shipped to the American colonies. As with many imported items, local tradesmen and artists soon began to produce their own versions. In the 1950s and 1960s, American companies such as Plymouth, Nashco, Pilgrim, and Fine Arts Studio brought about a resurgence in the demand for these fine collectibles.

Some collectors seek only chinoiserie designs, mother-of-pearl inlays, rose motifs, or specimens of a certain hue or from a particular country of origin. Tray prices can range from less than one hundred to thousands of dollars, depending upon age, condition, subject matter, and quality of painting.

Many stunning examples of toleware are available, although items without damage are becoming increasingly difficult to find. A toleware collection is a wonderful way to add elegance and warmth to home décor, perhaps with an array of trays hung on a wall, an oversize selection placed above a mantel, or a lovely tableau arranged on a coffee table with flowers and a candle.

Sterling TRADITIONS

Polished to a lustrous sheen, silver adds a hallmark of grace to the table. Mixing her signature pattern with prized heirlooms and other collected treasures, this seasoned hostess sets the scene for celebration.

For Elizabeth McGiffert, as the sun sets on Thanksgiving Day, thoughts shift from sharing a casual harvest meal on the family farm to planning a festive and formal Christmas Eve dinner at home. The McGiffert brothers and their wives alternate serving as hosts for this grand occasion, and when it is Elizabeth's turn to welcome loved ones to the table, place settings gleam with the timeless allure of precious metals.

"Sterling silver is classic and elegant," she says. "I appreciate it for its beauty but also because every piece has a story behind it." Pulling objets d'art from her custom-built

THE CARE OF STERLING SILVER

Although some antiques should be given to the care of a professional, these tips can help keep a collection in prime condition.

➤ Rotate displays to avoid exposure to sunlight, heat, and humidity.
➤ Promptly after use, hand-wash silver and dry with a soft cotton cloth.
➤ Wrapping items in specially treated flannel prevents flatware from tarnishing during storage.
➤ Use reputable products and gentle tools when polishing is needed.
➤ Scouring silver pieces rigorously may irreparably damage the finish. Employ mild techniques with delicate objects, and accept the warmth of patina.

silver closet, each loving cup, bonbon dish, and compote seems to hold memories. She recalls an instant attraction to many of her finds. In fact, when she spotted a folding biscuit box online, she was so overcome by its rarity that she claimed the hinged basket immediately and then breathed a sigh of relief when her husband also agreed to the purchase. A shapely punch bowl captivated her at Atlanta's famed Scott Antique Markets but has become even more precious over years of use.

Particular makers connect Elizabeth to some significant women in her life. A Gorham Chantilly collection passed down from her grandmother evokes fond remembrances of the beloved matriarch, while Towle Louis XIV flatware engraved with an *E* reminds her of the late friend whose son entrusted her with his mother's silver. Reed & Barton Francis I, with its voluminous scrollwork and exquisite fruit and flowers, is doubly special to Elizabeth now that she and her daughter both collect the Renaissance-inspired pattern.

Although frequent entertaining ensures that her finery is enjoyed often—"My mother always says that you can never go wrong with using nice things," she says—Christmastime offers the perfect opportunity to reflect the joy of the season in sterling silver.

OF *Rest* & RESTORATION

In a journey that reads more like a novel than a business plan, Pandora de Balthazár has followed her heart from a bucolic childhood in the Deep South, across oceans to distant palaces, and back home to discover her true purpose.

Pandora de Balthazár, founder of the luxury bedding company that bears her name, has been known to linger for hours with guests who visit her retail space in Pensacola, Florida. In a role she describes as equal parts interior designer and therapist, the former financial planner now helps clients invest in their own well-being.

With roots in Dalton, Georgia, which she calls the "textile capital of the new world," Pandora grew up with an appreciation for the handmade. She compares her rural upbringing, where from a tender age she was trained to sew and embroider, with the traditional education common to generations of young women who were raised abroad.

During her international travels, Pandora amassed an impressive collection of linens, prized as much for their practicality as for their artistry. She learned to distinguish antique from vintage textiles. Finely wrought pieces boast a heavier weight and superior craftsmanship, she notes. Realistic motifs rendered in meticulous stitches typify these valuable finds, which often tell a story.

In the midst of a successful corporate career, a serious automobile accident taught the jet-setting adviser the importance of creating a personal sanctuary. Following medical treatment in Hungary, Pandora convalesced for six months within a lavish nineteenth-century castle, where she realized the restorative power of sleep. Much of the healing she credits to cushions arranged to cradle her frame—a precursor to the European Sleep System she later developed.

In 1995, Pandora had just returned to the states when, again, her life shifted dramatically. Her family's beachfront house and almost all of their possessions were lost when Hurricane Opal struck Pensacola. With no idea where the path would lead, Pandora took a leap of faith when a woman who had heard about her Hungarian pillows invited her to become a vendor at High Point Market, the largest trade show in the furnishings industry.

More than twenty years after that initial endeavor, the Pandora de Balthazár company offers an ethereal selection of antique and custom-made sheets, shams, coverlets, and tablecloths, as well as foundational elements for the boudoir. Merchandise can be perused at prominent antiques shows around the country, as well as at the business's Florida location.

The purveyor of European linens encourages customers to embrace a more graceful way of living. "So many women need to be nurtured, and they don't even know it," she says—a lesson Pandora learned years ago, and a gift she shares with all who seek repose amidst her exquisite wares.

Vessels FROM THE PAST

A well-worn patina and interior glaze identify the shapely containers that were used for centuries to transport perishable goods around the Mediterranean. Today, these antique treasures can be found in gardens and also within the home, adding a touch of history and a unique focal point to any space.

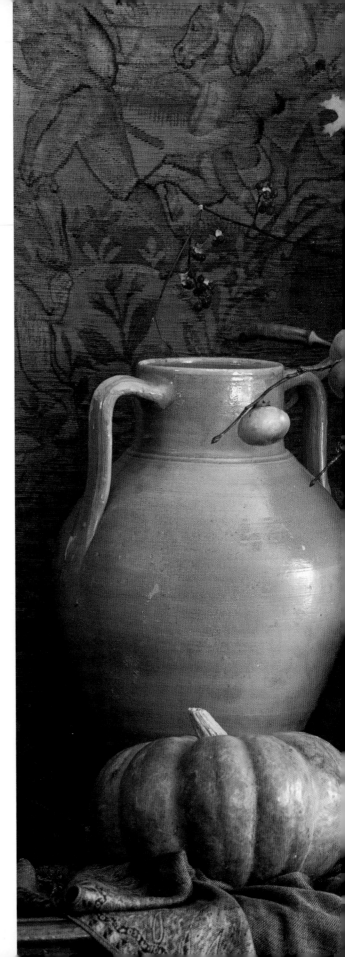

Myriad shades of earthenware seem to perfectly mirror the red and orange hues dotting treetops in the late weeks of the harvest season. Darker clays and vibrant yellow glazes remind one of the breathtaking landscape that typifies that time of year, but even the paler varieties have seen hundreds of colorful autumns since their creation.

A staple of European trade between the sixteenth and nineteenth centuries, these hefty terra-cotta basins were used to house both wet and dry food goods while being shipped throughout the region. Several styles exist, created by manufacturers from Spain to Turkey.

One iconic type is the Biot jar, named after the small town in southeastern France where hundreds of thousands of vessels were produced and exported as far as America and the coast of India. Still known today as Potter's Village, Biot sits on a hilltop south of Nice, mere miles from the sea.

Olive jugs bearing the name of this commune are typically large—more than three feet in height—with a shape much like the Mediterranean fruit they often carried. Pottery of this size was not crafted on a wheel but by using an ancient technique called the rope-thrown method. After winding ropes around a wooden framework, artisans applied wet clay to the outside, smoothing the surface and waiting for the formation to dry prior to removing the structure, which left a beautiful horizontal pattern inside. The interior and neck were glazed before firing in order to protect the terra-cotta from absorbing any oil it might store.

Our assortment, consisting of pieces mostly from the late eighteenth century, includes these classic French jars, as well as some other variations with distinct characteristics, such as handles, spigots, glaze drips, and even maker's marks. Each of these features is rare and sought after by collectors who decorate both home and garden with these uniquely textured antiques.

Endless PATTERN PLAY

When a transplanted Brit hosted an open house to celebrate royal nuptials, her guests admired the merry mix of English china she chose for the table settings. She turned that artful idea into a thriving business.

In the early morning hours of April 29, 2011, Vanessa Gilbreath and friends gathered at her Marietta, Georgia, home to watch the fairy-tale wedding of Britain's Prince William and his bride, Kate Middleton. As a native of Guildford in Surrey, this English expatriate knew the occasion called for a grand fête, and the tables were dressed to perfection with treasures inherited from her grandmother and great aunt.

Vanessa's guests were delighted to dine on such exquisite dinnerware and asked their hostess, "Why don't we do this more often?" That simple question sparked an idea for a business, and as soon as her companions bade her goodbye, she sat down at the computer to explore her options. While many companies rented tableware for events, Vanessa couldn't help but notice it wasn't fine china. Knowing that England had virtually unlimited sources for classic floral patterns, like those gracing her own table, she realized she'd found her niche, and her business Vintage English Teacup was born.

During visits home to the U.K., Vanessa continues to expand her vast inventory, scouring Spode and Wedgwood factory stores and attending country house auctions, where the best finds happen during inclement weather when the competition is minimal. Arriving at a centuries-old house in the English countryside on a cold, rainy day, she might have low expectations about what waits within, only to brush back a layer of straw in an old wooden chest to find a treasure trove of plates to join her abundant cache back in the states.

Though Vanessa supplies china for a wide variety of affairs, she often partners with Alexis Amaden, who operates the circa 1900 Whitlock Inn, a residence–turned–events venue, located near Marietta Square, the town's popular shopping and dining district. With its pretty façade, leaded-glass windows, and verdant grounds brimming with daffodils, dogwoods, and azaleas, the home is the ideal backdrop for weddings and other special occasions. In this sublime setting, Vanessa's medley of splendidly mismatched pieces is a sweet reminder of that spring day many years ago when a prince wed his beloved and charmed the world.

Graceful GRANDEUR

Our personal treasures—those thoughtfully acquired pieces that create a mood or call to mind a special memory—suffuse interiors with heart and soul. Humble or history-steeped, these are the objects that make a home.

CATCHING THE LIGHT

In classic fairy-tale fashion, a designer's touch awakens a long-neglected property, restoring warmth and beauty to its storybook cottage and coaxing a barren landscape to blossom as never before.

Banks of 'Limelight' hydrangeas, with their profusion of enormous chartreuse blooms, roll out a vibrant welcome to the Columbus, Georgia, home of Marsha Mason. Brimful annual and perennial beds envelop her 1926 Tudor charmer—its visage softened by verdant tendrils of creeping fig clambering up the façade and a canopy of fragrant New Dawn roses that stretches over the front porch. Window boxes spilling over with lemon cypress, 'Macho' fern, and ivy invite a peek inside, where sun-washed quarters convey the same exuberance as the lush surroundings.

Surveying Marsha's house and gardens, it is difficult to believe that this vision of seasonal splendor ever

languished. But when the Masons discovered the cottage in 2001, the interior decorator recalls that it was in terrible condition. "From the street, it looked like a big brick rectangle with no curb appeal," she says. "I only had the courage to show one friend. I kept everyone else away until it was renovated."

On the day of purchase, every living room window was hidden behind shutters, sheers, and curtains. "The first thing I did," she says, "was pull it all down." Over nine months, the family worked within the dwelling's original footprint to reconfigure an awkward layout. With a better flow established, Marsha was able to flood dark, dreary corners with natural light. She sewed new drapes and coated walls in cheery hues. Furnished with antiques, artwork, and collectibles, revitalized spaces became favorite spots to linger.

"You can tell so much about the personality of homeowners by what they are drawn to," says Marsha, who believes that collections offer the easiest and most interesting path to customizing a residence. Along with a bounty of blue-and-white Staffordshire transferware, she displays artwork, family photos, and Herend figures in artful groupings. The antiques enthusiast encourages giving pride of place to objects that are imbued with special memories. "Just like there isn't another you in this world," she adds, "your home should look only like you."

For this designer, color remains an enduring inspiration. Although she can appreciate the serenity of a neutral palette, in her own environs, Marsha finds joy among vivid yellows, greens, and blues punctuated with bright accents of coral or salmon. "No matter where I travel, I am always happy to come home to my little cottage," she says. "I hope it is as welcoming to others as it is to me."

Reclaiming
LOST CHARM

*After many years of hiding behind a
curtain of overgrown shrubbery, a
quintessential Southern vernacular house
has been lovingly restored by a talented couple
who helped the neglected property regain its
place as a much-admired residence.*

When Jamie Harris first drove by an 1830s raised cottage set on several acres, she could barely discern the outlines of a porch behind a tangle of brambles and bushes—but she could tell the house had character. Some years later, when she heard it was coming up for sale, she quickly arranged a visit before the listing officially went on the market. As it happens, Jamie and her husband, Rob, were leaving that day for a trip to Italy, but they were so taken with the property, they made an offer from the airport. Happily, it was accepted.

The Harrises were no strangers to renovations, having owned a number of old or historic homes that required varying degrees of repair—most notably the Virginia farmhouse where Rob had

grown up—but nothing matched the scale of this project. They worked with an architect and a builder who shared their commitment to honoring the integrity of the structure.

Fortunately, the layout was nearly perfect, and few structural changes were needed. A previous renovation in the 1930s bestowed its own lovely touches on the dwelling while blending beautifully with original features. Ceilings soar to nearly twelve feet, and a mix of oak and pine floors are unified with a dark stain. There are seven fireplaces; one has a mantel that dates to the seventeenth century and another most likely served a summer kitchen.

The interiors Jamie saw in Italy inspired the soft neutral palette she has used throughout her

own spaces. "I love the way the plaster walls, mouldings, and ceilings were all painted the same color there," she explains. "I chose to do that in most rooms of this house, which shows off the architecture so beautifully—and it allows the patina of the antiques to show." As an avid collector, she has acquired a wonderful mélange of time-brushed pieces, from English and French furniture to creamware, majolica, tapestry fragments, and more.

Bringing the cottage back to life has been a meaningful experience for Jamie and her family, as well as to the community as a whole. "We have so many neighbors that comment about being able to see the house again—almost everyone has a personal memory of the property," she says. "For now, it is our home, and the children love it as much as we do. After many moves, I believe this is the home they will remember the most."

Entwined MEMORIES

When a former governor and his family relocated to the sylvan surroundings of northern Virginia, they brought with them their Midwestern values and heritage, as well as an accumulated cache of heirloom antiques and cherished memorabilia.

I n a quiet suburban neighborhood just outside Washington, D.C., a stone-clad Colonial-style residence nestles amid a bevy of mature hardwood trees, their leaves tinged with the first golden hues of autumn. The beautifully landscaped garden, with an idyllic waterfall and lush plantings, offers a peaceful refuge from the bustling capital city nearby. It's a setting well-earned by the couple who reside here.

"The homeowners have deep roots in the business and political life of the Midwest, as well as multi-generational family histories there," relates their interior designer, Anne Dutcher, who has worked with these clients since 2013 to achieve the layered look that so perfectly suits the refined and welcoming interiors. Though the home is just shy of twenty years old, a prized assemblage of thoughtfully curated antiques—some inherited, others procured—gives it a time-brushed patina that belies its tender age.

The wife's preference for warm tones and timeless style is evidenced throughout the spaces, as is her unerring eye for detail. Anne notes she is passionate about her collections, which range from Limoges boxes and sunflower pottery to a number of horse-themed articles dear to her heart. "After raising her family and enjoying a very successful career in law," the designer explains, "she has re-embraced her passion for competing in dressage riding."

A striking de Gournay silk wall covering featuring birds, flowers, and tree branches wraps around the dining room, where a brace of rooster lamps rests on the sideboard and a beaded chandelier glimmers above the table. One cannot help but notice the mesmeric array of fabrics in every area of the house, and in this room, an embroidered pattern adorns the front and back of the chairs, while a buff-colored Ultrasuede covers their seats. The mahogany-paneled library also benefits from luxe materials; its coziness is due in part to the textured Ralph Lauren fabric installed on the ceiling.

The kitchen renovation three years ago was one of Anne's favorite projects, which included handmade tiles and hand-forged hardware. The adjoining breakfast room is especially spectacular, with a faux-painted ceiling by decorative artisan and muralist Bryan King as its crowning glory. He has contributed other works that add to the bespoke nature of this couple's thoroughly gracious home, which is a true reflection of the two. "They are both interesting people and have such great taste," says Anne. "Working with them and getting to know them over the years has been really lovely."

New England CLASSIC

Summer settles into the amiable village of Essex, Connecticut, where whispers of gentle breezes and the cheerful lilt of birdsong serve as background music to this much-anticipated season. Amid the floral fanfare, one residence stands out for its enviable beauty, both indoors and out.

British-born antiques dealer Shirley Kaplan had always dreamed of living in a stone house among the meandering hills of her homeland's Cotswolds region, so when she and husband Burt came across the gambrel Colonial in Essex, it was love at first sight. The dwelling was constructed for a local shipbuilder in 1790 on an elevated site with views to the Connecticut River so he could watch his ships' arrivals and departures.

Ensconced in a verdant, acre-plus setting, the home is a vision of pure New England charm, with traditional clapboard siding painted a soft buttermilk hue and burgundy awnings perched over first-floor windows. Many of the original features, including five fireplaces, remain intact, and hardwood gleams on every floor, framing a splendid array of handmade rugs.

Furnishing such an extraordinary property might have been a bit daunting, but the Kaplans knew just where to start. "A house speaks to you and tells you what it wants," says Shirley. "You just need to listen." The centuries-old walls appealed to the couple's affection and admiration for things steeped in history, and a thoughtful assemblage of antiques throughout the rooms reflects this love—an interest so keen that it became their business.

For a number of years, the Kaplans have been associated with Avery & Dash, a gallery in nearby Stamford that offers period furniture similar to the pieces that imbue their own home with timeworn elegance. For ten years, the couple also owned a storefront enterprise named English Accents, but they closed it to focus on the gallery operation and to allow more time for travel.

"The pieces we favor are those with quiet charm and great patina and color," explains Shirley. "They make you want to reach out and lightly run your fingertips over their well-loved surfaces." A perfect example is the grand, circa 1800 Welsh dresser that she and Burt found on one of their many buying trips to England. The dresser holds her priceless collection of majolica.

Equally as beautiful as the interiors, the grounds are a collaborative effort between husband and wife. Shirley designed the layout of the plot, but both have pitched in to create a quintessential English cottage garden that would be quite at home across the pond.

"I've always loved roses and have them throughout the property," says Shirley. "Also, I feel a cutting garden is a necessity, and I intersperse mine with herbs and vegetables." Wisteria, honeysuckle, and rambling roses soften the landscape while also imparting a sweetly mingled fragrance.

With the arrival of summer, Shirley and Burt welcome friends to gather amid the blooms, enjoying meals on the patio or taking a dip in the pool. And as the sunset paints the sky in brilliant hues, they will watch the ships return to port, just as the first seafaring owner did long ago.

STORIED TREASURES

A monthlong European cruise at age sixteen sparked a lifelong love affair for designer Lee Stough. The beauty of these foreign lands compels her to return, again and again, in search of inspiration.

Tucked into the verdant hills of Louisville, Kentucky, Lee Stough's classic Tudor home evokes thoughts of cozy European country houses with proper pedigrees. Inside each room, streams of light land on carefully culled collections from her various trips abroad.

Having grown up in Charlottesville, Virginia, a city where everyday life is influenced by the legacy of Thomas Jefferson, the noted statesman and a great European traveler in his own right, Lee's childhood included exposure to the four corners of the globe. Touring with her grandparents throughout Iceland, Scandinavia, Russia, and England opened her eyes to the wonders of these nations. College treks across France and Italy fully cemented this adoration and beckoned her back as often as possible—even for just a week's vacation—to the lands she loved.

A fourth-grade paper written on Jacqueline Kennedy's renovation of the White House first piqued Lee's interest in interior design. Impressed by all she had seen in the regions, homes, and museums she had explored around the world, studying art history in college was a natural progression. Later, having moved to New York City to live near the center of the design industry, and benefiting from the opportunity to wander through the endless art galleries there, Lee furthered her education by obtaining a degree from the New York School of Interior Design.

After working in the field for fifteen years, Lee established her own design business centered on her personal philosophy that a home should be both a sanctuary and a haven. She assists her clients in creating environments of comfort and contentment that reflect their own interests and experiences. Working out of a studio she shares with two other designers, Lee reserves her home as a space for creativity and dreaming.

Her design concepts originate from her vast collection of memories and past journeys, as well as from those she continues to make. According to Lee, "Experiencing

another way of life and learning from it is one of the most invaluable ways I seek inspiration."

Recollections of vibrant market days in the village of Saint-Rémy-de-Provence, the air filled with the scent of lavender and rosemary; wandering Magazine Street in New Orleans, the shops brimming with treasures brought over from France, England, and Italy—all have influenced the choices Lee makes for her clients' residences. Borrowing from the palettes of the sun-bleached villages of Provence and the gently worn frescoes of an ancient Italian church, she uses these time-tested colors and textures to add an intangible richness to the bank of ideas from which she draws.

In Lee's words, "Whether it is an upholstered wall, a painted finish, or a piece of porcelain, there are always visual souvenirs that serve to energize me. I love my home—I love being at home—and my goal is for my clients to experience that same sort of bliss."

Where Loveliness Lives

Learning to embrace her light-filled home's unique contours and qualities inspired one owner to create tranquil interiors where her lovingly curated collections and antique furnishings truly have the space to shine.

When contractor Price McGiffert bought an unusual, octagon-shaped house in the neighborhood where his wife had grown up, his initial plan was to remodel and sell it. But somewhere in the process, it became clear to him that this could be the perfect residence for their family of five. Convincing his spouse of that was another matter.

"Though I'd loved that house all my life, I thought I was already living in my dream home," says Elizabeth, "but Price is very talented, and he could visualize its potential." What followed was a thoughtfully planned renovation that respected the character of the original architecture while adding more square footage and features important to the couple and their children. Since all the previous rooms were octagonal, the new rooms were as well—something that might have presented a problem for some families when it came to furniture placement.

Through the years, Elizabeth has acquired a marvelous cache of antiques and Oushak rugs, as well as an enviable mélange of collections, from French jardinières and Rose Medallion porcelain to the large assemblage of sterling silver that is featured on page 72. She smiles and explains, "My mother and my grandmother both love beautiful things, so it was bound to rub off on me." One of her first pieces was a painted French wall cabinet that fits perfectly against one of the eight living room walls and showcases some of her favorite treasures.

For the past two decades, Elizabeth has worked with interior designer Harriet Adams to feather nests that are both elegant and timeless but also exceedingly livable. "By now, Harriet knows me so well," she relates, "she will see something and know it has my name written all over it." The designer's biannual trips to Europe have yielded cherished finds, including antique French balance scales in the kitchen

and a circa 1850 French Napoleon III marble–and–gilt bronze cassolette urn lamp for the study that was so exquisite, Elizabeth fell in love the second she saw it.

Light floods the home and, when coupled with the soft color palette, lends an ethereal serenity throughout. Every mesmeric space bears this gracious owner's aesthetic imprint, from the gorgeous furnishings in the living room to an early nineteenth-century hand-painted Aubusson cartoon in the master bath. Even if she resisted the move at first, Elizabeth has come to believe this is exactly where she was always meant to be.

Devotion TO HERITAGE

A treasure trove of lovingly curated antiques and architectural accents imbues one couple's home with a time-burnished character that belies its young age. Each beautiful piece has a story that calls up happy memories for these keen collectors.

Most of the stately manors found in Jan and Stan Cash's historic neighborhood date to the early 1920s, when this eminent mountaintop enclave was founded. Such was the case with their previous residence, which came with the option to buy the wooded lot next door. They did just that and spent the next two decades traveling the world, gathering reams of design ideas, along with a wondrous cache of venerable relics, for the English-style cottage they built on that adjacent site fourteen years ago.

"Stan says I've been planning this house all my life—and I really have," says Jan, who parlayed a love of history passed down from her father, along with the attention to detail and a penchant for beauty learned at her mother's knee, into a successful career as an interior designer. "Fate and a passion for collecting and selling antiques, as well as a lifelong appreciation for architecture and interiors, made this move inevitable."

The couple relied on internationally noted architects Bobby McAlpine and Greg Tankersley to

design a home that brought together all the elements, both conceptual and tangible, that they had been nurturing for years. Though McAlpine deemed the plot "difficult and challenging," he reassured the Cashes the daunting topography would not deter their plans.

It was important to Jan and Stan to incorporate natural materials in the design. Pecky cypress was used for ceilings, paneling, and doors, while old oak trees felled in the construction process were milled for beams throughout the spaces—a fortuitous outcome that especially pleased Stan. Floors are a mix of wood and stone. "The materials used have a timeless quality," says Jan, "and they were called for by the style of the house, the antiques within, and the historic neighborhood." Once the last driveway brick was laid, an enchanting abode blending Cotswolds charm with European elegance was nestled into its hillside haven.

The interiors are truly awe-inspiring. These dedicated collectors have surrounded themselves with a magnificent assemblage of antiquities found on their global travels, from ancient tapestries and ecclesiastical art to seashells and Palissy ware. The pieces lend the décor a time-brushed patina, and each room, every nook and corner, is an authentic reflection of both husband and wife and their mutual interests.

"At this point, nothing new can come in unless something else goes out," Jan explains. "Unfortunately, there is no room left for new treasures—although I hope I never lose my passion for the search."

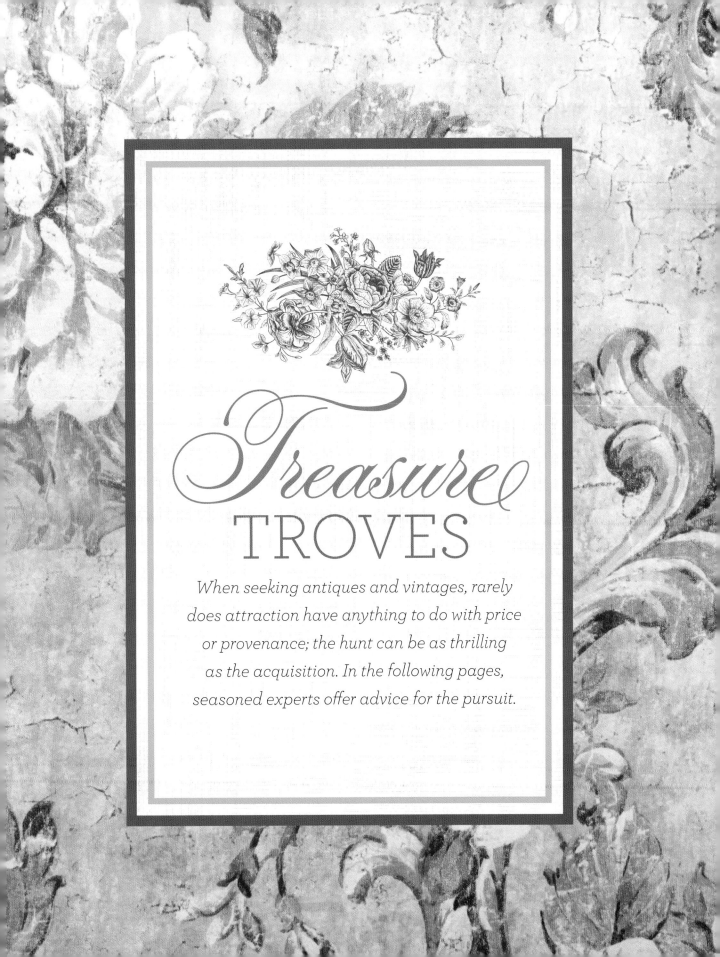

Treasure TROVES

When seeking antiques and vintages, rarely does attraction have anything to do with price or provenance; the hunt can be as thrilling as the acquisition. In the following pages, seasoned experts offer advice for the pursuit.

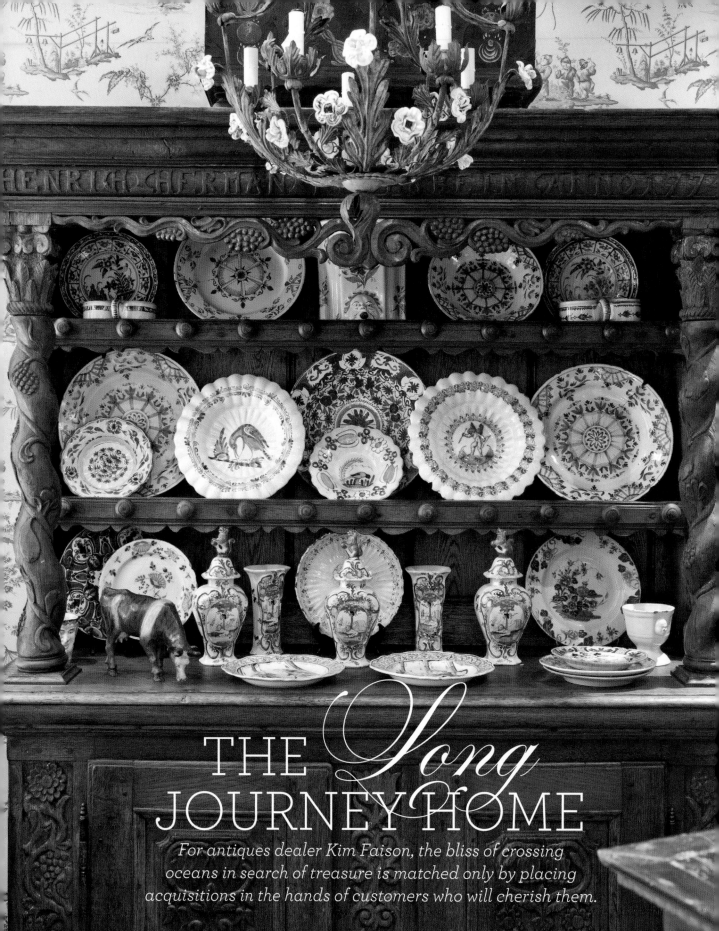

THE *Long* JOURNEY HOME

For antiques dealer Kim Faison, the bliss of crossing oceans in search of treasure is matched only by placing acquisitions in the hands of customers who will cherish them.

As Scandinavian merchants unload trucks at the Stockholm Furniture & Light Fair in Sweden, Kim Faison is there, perusing the wares. The only American (she hails from Richmond, Virginia) invited to preview these troves of Gustavian heirlooms, Kim will have come and gone long before the show opens to the public. This early morning scene is repeated throughout Europe as colleagues recognize in her a kindred spirit.

Often, Kim already has a specific client in mind when she spies a pièce de résistance. "It is an incredible joy to be so far away, find something exquisite, and know that a friend has the ideal spot for it," she says. Through Kim Faison Antiques, the entrepreneur has been connecting homeowners with seventeenth-, eighteenth-, and nineteenth-century furnishings for almost thirty years.

The appreciation for classic silhouettes, quality construction, and rich patina is a heritage passed down from her mother, Caroline Faison, an importer of fine Continental antiques. Kim apprenticed with her mom in Greensboro, North Carolina, for a decade before launching a career in Virginia.

When Kim's younger son started kindergarten, she opened her eponymous shop in a 900-square-foot bungalow set within walking distance of her boys' school. Later, the business moved across the street to a circa 1926 house nearly three times the size of the original cottage—a gracious locale for showcasing a wide array of furniture, pottery, and accessories from around the world.

Despite the splendor Kim observes during buying trips abroad, she says that nothing compares with coming back and beholding her own inventory with fresh eyes. When she revisits clients, she can't help whispering a greeting as she runs her hands over previous finds—recalling instantly the day she found each piece, precisely where it was displayed, and how much she paid for it. "Antiques are like my children," she says. "They might be living in a new home, but they will always be mine."

Cultivating
A LOVE FOR ANTIQUES

A trusted dealer of fine French furniture and source for rare and unusual pieces, most notably those from the seventeenth to nineteenth centuries, shares her insights on making the most of shopping at renowned antiques fairs and shows.

The prospect of navigating large fairs might seem overwhelming to a novice, so we turned to antiques dealer Mary Helen McCoy to demystify the process. She offers sage advice for collecting sought-after pieces, working with trustworthy vendors, and negotiating a fair price.

Mary Helen believes that collecting takes time and is a process based on personal taste. She suggests starting with a collection of small items, such as picture frames, boxes, or teacups. "Collect pieces that really appeal to you, regardless of what other people like," she advises. "And, no matter what your budget is, you should search for the best you can possibly afford and take your time to gather the best pieces."

ROUND TOP ANTIQUES FAIR

➤ Having celebrated its golden anniversary in 2018, this show draws collectors to rural Texas three times per year. The extensive variety includes early American primitives, fine European textiles, ancient prints, architectural salvage, and porcelain. The Big Red Barn houses thirty thousand square feet of Americana and Continental pieces, and Marburger Farm features more than 350 dealers with high-end antiques.

Because identifying age and authenticity can be complicated, Mary Helen emphasizes the importance of working with reputable dealers. She recommends becoming familiar with collectible items by attending museum exhibits and studying reference books, but ultimately trusting a dealer. "The best place to educate your eye is at a show," she says, "where you can actually touch and feel the pieces and learn the difference between what is merely decorative and what is a true antique."

Before picking up a centuries-old ceramic bowl or sitting down on a valuable antique chair, ask the dealer for permission. "Really respect the furniture and accessories," Mary Helen says. "Dealers are happy for you to touch, but let them show you how, so that you don't throw off a drawer or force open a lock." She points out that an excellent dealer will always demonstrate a willingness to teach and engage in conversation. "If you're not greeted kindly or treated well in a booth, then you should move along to the next one," Mary Helen adds.

BRIMFIELD ANTIQUE FLEA MARKETS

➤ Every May, July, and September, thousands of treasure hunters converge on the tiny community of Brimfield, Massachusetts, to seek out everything from fine and rare antique furniture to kitschy vintage collectibles. Arguably the most famous antiques exhibition in the United States, the show began in 1959 and has since become a mecca for savvy dealers, serious shoppers, and casual collectors alike.

Likewise, dealers may not be interested in working with someone who asks them first, "What is your best price?" Although they do expect some bartering, leading with a question about money indicates that a person is shopping by price only. "The best questions to ask a dealer are: 'What is this?' 'Where did it come from?' 'How old is it?' 'Has there been any restoration?'" Mary Helen says.

Her final advice? "Just relax, and don't be intimidated by what you see at a show—we were all novices once." Even with decades of experience, Mary Helen still enjoys simply perusing the beautiful, historical pieces each show has to offer.

SCOTT ANTIQUE MARKETS

➤ Held monthly in Atlanta, Georgia, and at various times throughout the year in Columbus, Ohio, this family-owned and -operated business comprising four generations has grown over thirty years to become what is now the world's largest monthly indoor antiques show. Attendees can peruse a wide selection of silver, pottery, fine crystal, period furniture, memorabilia, and much more.

FRENCH TRANSLATION

Kathy Delgado achieved success in corporate America, but the proprietor of Vintageweave Interiors found true fulfillment when she followed her heart to Europe.

As a senior vice president for a commercial real estate developer, Kathy Delgado graced magazine covers and was listed among the most powerful women in her profession nationwide. But even though the Los Angeles–based executive had attained wealth, prestige, and numerous accolades, daydreams carried her far away from this competitive business environment.

On weekend escapes to Europe, Kathy indulged her passion for romantic French ambiance—exploring

Parisian flea markets and pausing to savor buttered croissants. One day, she got lost and entered a small antiques store to ask for directions. Without success, she tried to communicate with the French-speaking owners, pointing to the address in her notes. To Kathy's surprise, the older couple took her hands and gently led her from the shop, pausing to turn the sign on the door to "Closed" before walking her to the destination. Experiencing this generosity of spirit only deepened her longing for a different career path.

Back in California, entertainment-industry clients noticed the French treasures that lined Kathy's office shelves and began inquiring about pieces for their productions. Dinner party guests encouraged her to pursue interior decorating, and she helped design her company's new headquarters. Gradually, a clear vision emerged. "I was yearning for my creative self to come to the forefront," she says.

Kathy admits that the idea of leaving the security of a job she enjoyed was daunting. She credits the advice of a Hollywood director with giving her the push she needed.

"Don't confuse money with your life's calling," he urged. "You've made your fortune. Now let that be the vehicle that helps you launch your dream."

In 2005, Kathy founded Vintageweave Interiors, a Los Angeles haven of authentic French-farmhouse antiques and home décor. Although she operates mainly by private appointment, she opens the shop to the public during select hours and sells worldwide through the company's website. With her showroom steps away from a network studio, Kathy also consults on set design and cooking-show prop styling. Her wares were featured in Tim Burton's cinematic adaptation of Lewis Carroll's *Alice in Wonderland*.

The entrepreneur is grateful to have found both a career and a calling in Vintageweave. "I can't properly put into words how enthusiastic I am about getting up every day," Kathy says.

Old-World
ELEGANCE

Tucked amid the more than three hundred stores composing the prestigious Dallas Design District is an emporium replete with a heart-stirring array of classic and unforgettable European antiques.

S trolling through the massive showroom at Inessa Stewart's Antiques & Interiors in Texas is akin to visiting one of the great palaces of Europe, with ornate gilded mirrors, marble-top tables, and carved mahogany beds at every turn. Ecclesiastical items, from Madonna figures to prayer benches, mingle with French faience plates and gleaming copper pots. This destination is an antiques aficionado's dream—and a dream come true for the owner.

"My passion for history and antiques began as a child when my mother and I would attend museums,

art galleries, opera, ballet, and theatre," says Inessa, who spent her childhood in the Black Sea port city of Odessa. "Being steeped in such a rich cultural heritage made a profound impression, and to this day, I strive to re-create that magic everywhere I can."

And the store is a magical place, a gallimaufry of furniture and accessories representing numerous periods and countries of origins, with styles ranging from refined to rustic. Inessa and her husband, John, have cultivated close relationships with dealers across Europe, and the couple handpicks every piece of inventory. "Being passionate about what we do, we look at each treasure as collectors first and as antiques dealers second," she explains, "because we know that each piece will soon become a precious part of our clients' lives, starting a new chapter in the story of their home."

The Stewarts operate a second brick-and-mortar location in Baton Rouge, as well as a thriving online business. These offerings have connected them with interior designers all over the world.

Every space, Inessa contends, shines brighter with the patina of age. "Placing at least one old piece per room adds a layer of visual interest and makes an interior come to life," says Inessa. "Antiques touch your soul as they become a part of your everyday home life."

CREDITS & RESOURCES

The Art of Collecting

Editor-in-Chief: Phyllis Hoffman DePiano
Editor: Melissa Lester
Senior Director of Design and Brand Development:
Melissa Sturdivant Smith
Associate Editors:
Karen Callaway, Leslie Bennett Smith
Assistant Editor: Kassidy Abernathy
Art Director: Tracy Wood-Franklin
Editorial Assistant: Lydia McMullen
Creative Director/Photography: Mac Jamieson
Photographers:
John O'Hagan, Stephanie Welbourne Steele
Senior Copy Editor: Rhonda Lee Lother
Senior Digital Imaging Specialist: Delisa McDaniel

CONTRIBUTING WRITERS

KASSIDY ABERNATHY: page 35
LIDY BAARS: pages 68–71
J. R. BERNO: pages 146–151
KAREN CALLAWAY: pages 12–15, 24–27, 36–39, 46–49,
    64–67, 88–93, 102–119, and 126–139
BRITTANY WILLIAMS FLOWERS: pages 120–125
KATE CARTER FREDERICK: pages 18–23
CATHERINE HAMRICK: pages 16–17
KIMBER MITCHELL: pages 28–33
STACEY NORWOOD: pages 52–57

NANCY A. RUHLING: pages 58–63
LESLIE BENNETT SMITH: pages 40–45 and 84–87

CONTRIBUTING PHOTOGRAPHERS

GAYLE BROOKER: pages 25 and 27
CARYN B. DAVIS: pages 114–119
KIMBERLY FINKEL DAVIS: pages 10, 16–17, 20–22, 94, and
    120–125
BRITTANY WILLIAMS FLOWERS: pages 8, 140, and 146–149
KATE SEARS: pages 50 and 52–57
CYNTHIA SHAFFER: pages 68–71
MARCY BLACK SIMPSON: pages 24, 26, 32, 34–39, 46–49,
    61–67, 142–145, and 152–157

CONTRIBUTING STYLISTS

LIDY BAARS: pages 68–71
SIDNEY BRAGIEL: pages 32, 34–39, 42–45, and 102–107
MISSIE NEVILLE CRAWFORD: pages 2, 64–67 and 78–83
ANNE DUTCHER: pages 108–113
BRITTANY WILLIAMS FLOWERS: pages 50, 52–57, 94, and
    120–125
MARY LEIGH GWALTNEY: pages 28–33 and 36–39
YUKIE MCLEAN: pages 10, 16-17, 20–22, and 58–63
MELISSA STURDIVANT SMITH: Cover and pages 4–5,
    12–15, 18–19, 23–24, 26, 40–49, 72–77, 84–93, 126–139,
    and 158–161
KATHLEEN COOK VARNER: pages 2 and 78–83

WHERE TO SHOP & BUY

Below is a list of properties and companies featured in this book.

Pages 12–15: Maison de France Antiques, 1304 8th Street, Leeds, AL, 205-699-6330.

Pages 20–22: The Brown House: Antiques, Art, Comforts of Life, thebrownhouse.bigcartel.com.

Page 24: Wedgwood: Jasperware Jewelry Brooch, call for availability; from Replacements, Ltd., 800-737-5223, replacements.com.

Pages 24 & 26: Elise Abrams Antiques, 11 Stockbridge Road, Great Barrington, MA, 413-528-3201, eliseabramsantiques.com.

Pages 25 & 27: Amedeo, 946 Lexington Avenue, New York, NY, 212-737-4100, amedeo.shop.

Page 26: Extasia: Hand Carved Bone Pliny Dove Necklace; 530-292-9151, extasia.com.

Pages 28–33: Ashford Hill for Henhouse Antiques, 1900 Cahaba Road, Birmingham, AL, 205-918-0505, henhouseantiques.com.

Pages 36–39: Attic Antiques, 5620 Cahaba Valley Road, Birmingham, AL, 205-991-6887, atticantiquesal.com.

Pages 40–43: Special thanks to Courtney Hildebrand. Learn more about her collection at ringboxesgalore.net.

Pages 44–45: Foreign Affair International: Édouard Garnier Antique Prints, call for availability; 404-213-9251, foreignaffairintl.com. Sadek: Sevres Flat Cup & Saucer Set in Green, Sevres Flat Cup & Saucer Set in Peach, Sevres Dinner Plate in Green, Sevres Salad/ Dessert Plate in Blue, Sevres Flat Cup & Saucer Set in Blue, Sevres Salad/ Dessert Plate in Peach, Sevres Dinner Plate in Blue, Sevres Flat Cup & Saucer Set in Purple, call for availability; from Replacements, Ltd., 800-737-5223, replacements.com.

Pages 50 and 52–57: Paris Hotel Boutique, 415-305-7846, parishotelboutique.com.

Pages 64–67: Rose Ann Kendrick's booth (Dealer #77) can be found at Hanna Antiques Mall, 2424 7th Avenue South, Birmingham, AL, 205-323-6036, hannaantiques.com.

Pages 68–71: French Garden House, 8941 Atlanta Avenue, Suite 284, Huntington Beach, CA, 714-454-3231, frenchgardenhouse.com.

Pages 78–83: Pandora de Balthazár, 418 East Wright Street, Pensacola, FL, 850-434-5117, pandoradebalthazar.com.

Pages 84–87: Variety of antique olive jars from Adams Antiques & The Potager, 428 Main Avenue, Northport, AL, 205-200-1968, adamsantiquesandthepotager.com.

Pages 88–93: Vintage English Teacup, 2908 Katy Lane, Marietta, GA, 770-317-6216, vintageenglishteacup.com. The Whitlock Inn, 57 Whitlock Avenue, Marietta, GA, 770-428-1495, whitlockinn.com.

Pages 96–101: Marsha Mason, marsha@wildwooddesign.net, Instagram: @marshamason2.

Pages 98: Gullatte Associates, Inc., 1041 1st Avenue, Columbus, GA, 706-322-3620, gullatte.com.

Pages 108–113: Anne Dutcher Interiors, LLC, Great Falls, VA, 703-759-5171, annedutcherinteriors.com. Artifice, Inc., 1829 North Quesada Street, Arlington, VA, 703-626-7900, artificeinc.com.

Pages 114–119: Avery & Dash, 101 Jefferson Street, Stamford, CT, 203-325-8070, averydash.com.

Pages 126–131: Harriet Adams, Adams Antiques & The Potager, 428 Main Avenue, Northport, AL, 205-200-1968, adamsantiquesandthepotager.com. Special thanks to Gary Turner for floral styling, gary@indianhillscountryclub.net.

Pages 132–139: Architecture by McAlpine, 505 Cloverdale Road, Suite 102, Montgomery, AL, 334-262-8315, mcalpinehouse.com.

Pages 142–145: Kim Faison Antiques, 2111 Lake Avenue, Richmond, VA, 804-282-3736, kimfaisonantiques.com.

Pages 146–151: Mary Helen McCoy Fine French Antiques & Decorative Accessories, Memphis, TN, 901-786-8115. Round Top Antiques Fair, 475 Texas Highway 237 South, Carmine, TX, 512-237-4747, roundtoptexasantiques.com. Brimfield Antique Show, 106 Five Bridge Road, Brimfield, MA, 844-746-6610, brimfieldantiquefleamarket.com. Scott Antique Markets (Atlanta), North Building: 3650 Jonesboro Road Southeast, Atlanta, GA, 404-361-2000; South Building: 3850 Jonesboro Road Southeast, Atlanta, GA, 404-363-2299, scottantiquemarket.com.

Pages 152–157: Vintageweave Interiors, Inc., 7928 West 3rd Street, Los Angeles, CA, 805-364-2403, vintageweave.com.

Pages 158–161: Inessa Stewart's Antiques & Interiors, 1643 Dragon at Oak Lawn, Dallas, TX, 214-742-5800, inessa.com.